Cushing's Disease in Dogs

S. Kenrose

ISBN 978-145-281-2557

Contents

Chapter One: Introduction 5

Chapter Two: What is Cushing's Disease? 9

THREE TYPES 11

SUSCEPTIBLE BREEDS 13

Chapter Three: Symptoms 15

Chapter Four: Diagnosis 19

THE URINE CORTISOL:CREATININE RATIO (UC:CR) 19

LOW DOSE DEXAMETHASONE SUPPRESSION TEST 20

ACTH STIMULATION TEST 20

Chapter Five: Treatment 23

ADRENAL TUMORS 23

PITUITARY DEPENDENT 24

TREATMENT FOR IATROGENIC CUSHING'S 30

Chapter Six: Associated Medical Complications 33

HYPERTENSION 33

PYELONEPHRITIS AND URINARY CALCULI 33

DIABETES MELLITUS 34

PULMONARY THROMBOEMBOLISM 34

Chapter Seven: Feeding your Cushing's Dog a Natural Diet 35

Chapter Eight: Genetics and Inheritability 39

HOW INHERITABILITY WORKS 40

Chapter Nine: Do Vaccinations cause Cushing's Disease? 45

TITER TESTING—AN ALTERNATIVE TO VACCINES 48

Chapter Ten: Cheaper Treatment Options 51

SHOP AROUND FOR DRUGS 51

Appendix A: What is an Addisonian Crisis? 55

Appendix B: Definitions 57

Bibliography 63

Index 67

Chapter One: Introduction

When Jack, a potbellied 12-year-old German shepherd, hobbled into the examination room, my first thought was Cushing's disease. "He keeps on howling to go potty in the middle of the night," my client, Betty said. "And I have to refill his water bowl every hour. It's getting ridiculous!"

I asked Betty to get Jack up on the table. Jack's huge belly and spindly legs gave him the appearance of a beer barrel on legs. If it was Cushing's, the pot belly was from fat redistribution and fat was most likely also accumulating in other areas that weren't visible like his thorax, and his blood. Jack's spindly legs could be from muscle wasting—another hallmark of Cushing's.

"How is he on walks?" I asked.

"Oh, we don't go on walks any more, do we, Jack," Betty said, scratching the top of her dog's head. "He's getting too old...he can't walk a block without getting out of breath."

Alarm bells began to sound. Cushing's can affect respiration because of several factors joining together to make breathing difficult: pressure from fat accumulation in the stomach, liver enlargement, fat deposition in the thorax, and wasting of respiratory muscles. The excess cortisol in the blood also relaxes the abdominal ligaments and enlarges the liver, giving the dog a characteristic potbellied appearance. A closer examination revealed patches of hair loss and poor coat quality which were even on both sides.

"How's his appetite?" I asked.

"He's a beggar," Betty said. "If I let him, he would eat, and eat, and eat. He never seems to be full. I figured that's why he's getting fat."

I felt more and more confident that Cushing's was the cause. There could be many other reasons for the hormonal imbalance — there's good reason why Cushing's counterpart, Addison's disease, is known as "The Great Pretender": it can mimic a whole host of diseases. But Cushing's can sometimes be easier to pinpoint, especially with classic signs like a potbelly, polyphagia (increased appetite) polydipsia (excessive drinking) and polyuria (excessive urination). However, you can't look at a dog and definitively say "Cushing's." Getting a definitive diagnosis is a challenge at best, and even tests can be inconclusive.

I subjected Jack to a Complete Blood Count, urinalysis, and Blood Chemistry Panel. Results showed that Jack had high levels of cholesterol and blood glucose as well as extremely dilute urine. The blood tests also showed the presence of Alanine Transaminase (ALT), an enzyme that is leaked into the blood when liver cells are damaged, and high levels of alkaline phosphatase (AKP), another indicator of possible liver damage.

Aware that a definitive diagnosis of Cushing's Disease can't be reached based on laboratory tests alone, I asked Betty for permission to run additional tests, including an 8-hour Dexamethasone Suppression Test or Low-Dose Dexamethasone Suppression Test (you can read all about this test in Chapter Four: Diagnosis). To confirm that Jack was suffering from Cushing's, the classical signs that he was manifesting should be coupled with a consistent medical history.

At the end of the test, Jack's cortisol levels remained high. A High-Dose Dexamethasone Suppression Test showed that Jack had an inoperable pituitary tumor, but was lucky because we had probably caught the disease early enough to treat it with pharmaceuticals. At least, that was my hope. You see, Cushing's is not only a challenge to diagnose, but it can also be a challenge to treat. No two cases are the same, and no two animals react the same to any of the several treatments available to treat Cushing's. Symptomatic treatment for Jack improved his condition within a month, but I knew it would take many months to stabilize him completely, and even then—he would need to be watched closely by his owner over the coming years.

As a veterinarian, I rely not only on tests to monitor how a dog is doing—owner input is essential. With Cushing's disease, you—as a dog owner—are part of the treatment team. The more knowledge you have about the disease, the better chance your dog has of living a long and happy life.

Merliza Cabriles, D.V.M.

Chapter Two: What is Cushing's Disease?

In 1932, Harvey Cushing wrote about a then-untreatable Illness in people characterized by large amounts of cortisol, a natural steroid that's responsible for regulating a host of body functions (E. C. Feldman 1995). This disease came to be known as hyperadrenocorticism, or Cushing's disease. There are three known causes of Cushing's disease: a pituitary malfunction, an adrenal malfunction, or a type of man-made Cushing's, usually caused by over medicating another condition like skin disorders or Addison's disease.

Cortisol is produced by the adrenal glands, two small glands located at the top of the kidneys. However, while the adrenal glands are responsible for cortisol production, they aren't normally the underlying problem in the vast amount of Cushing's cases.

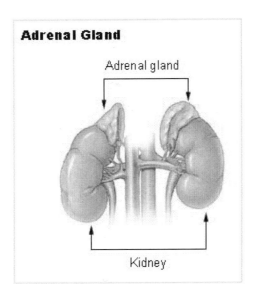

Adrenal Gland

Adrenal gland

Kidney

That distinction goes to the pituitary, a pea-sized gland located at the base of the brain.

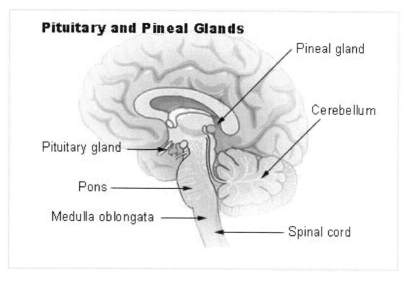

The pituitary gland produces a hormone called adrenocorticotropic hormone (ACTH), which sends a signal to the adrenal glands to produce cortisol. If too much ACTH is released into your dog's body, then too much cortisol will be released. Cortisol (along with another hormone, aldosterone), assists in regulating dozens of bodily functions, including:

- blood pressure
- cardiovascular function
- immune system inflammatory response
- insulin balance
- metabolism of proteins, carbohydrates, and fats

Perfectly balancing the amount of cortisol in the blood stream is vital for all round health. Usually, when levels of cortisol reach optimum level in the blood, the pituitary gland stops producing ACTH, which in turn signals the adrenal glands to stop producing cortisol. When cortisol levels drop too low, the pituitary gland releases ACTH again, signaling the adrenals to produce more cortisol. Ann Stohlman, V.M.D., a veterinarian at the FDA's Center for Veterinary Medicine, states that cortisol, in regular amounts, is beneficial. "It helps the body adapt in times of stress." However, if this delicate balancing act gets disturbed, then severe health problems ensue. Too little cortisol, and a dog can show signs of Addison's disease. Too much cortisol, and a dog can get Cushing's. Cushing's disease leads to a weakened immune system and can open your dog up to a slew of other diseases and disorders (U.S. Food and Drug Administration (FDA) 2009).

Three types

There are three main causes of canine Cushing's disease: pituitary-tumor (sometimes referred to as pituitary-dependent), adrenal cortical tumor, and iatrogenic (veterinarian-induced).

Pituitary Tumor

The vast majority of Cushing's cases (up to 85%) are caused by a tumor (or many microtumors) on the pituitary gland. The tumor causes ACTH to be overproduced, stimulating the adrenal glands to produce too much cortisol. According to Hahn (1997), a hallmark of this type of Cushing's is that both adrenal glands are enlarged at the same time.

Adrenal cortical tumor

Most of the other Cushing's cases are made up from a group with a tumor in one or the other adrenal gland. Unlike pituitary-dependent Cushing's, only one adrenal gland will become enlarged. In fact, one gland may be excessively large and the other excessively small (Hahn 1997).

Iatrogenic (veterinarian-induced)

Cushing's can be caused by over medicating certain illnesses with too much corticosteroid supplementation (Hines 2009). Some examples of other illnesses that might lead to iatrogenic Cushing's include excess cortisol being given to a dog with a skin disorder. If too much cortisol is given to the dog, the excess cortisol causes the pituitary gland to decrease the amount of cortisol released into the bloodstream. The adrenals—devoid of their usual level of cortisol manufacturing—decrease production and start to shrink (Hahn 1997).

This type of Cushing's is reversible with a lower dosage of medications (it's important not to completely stop administering cortisol because the dog's system has come to rely on it).

Susceptible Breeds

Dogs at high risk for Cushing's include:

- Silky Terriers
- Bull Terriers
- Boston Terriers
- Yorkshire terriers
- Dachshunds
- Poodles
- German Shepherds

The disease is most often seen in dogs over five years old. Although the mechanism isn't completely understood, females are more likely to have adrenal gland tumors than males (Hines 2009) (Hahn 1997).

Chapter Three: Symptoms

Cushing's disease isn't a disease that is plainly obvious to the dog owner (or even many veterinarians). The disease typically shows up in middle-aged to older dogs (though it can occur at any age), so the myriad of symptoms often mask themselves as the aging process. The symptoms may even occur so gradually that you might not notice them for months, or even years.

According to Michele Laurensen, DVM (Laurenson 2010) the most frequent signs of Cushing's disease are:

- Increased drinking and urination (polydipsia and polyuria) (80-91%). You might notice you have to fill your pet's water bowl more often, or you may notice they have to go to the bathroom more than usual.

- Hair loss (alopecia) (60-74%). Those thinning patches of hair on your pet may not be due to "old age." It's extremely common for Cushing's patients to have bald spots.

- "Barrel stomach" (pendulous abdomen) (67-73%). Cushing's disease dog owners often comment on their dogs' weight gain. However, hyperadrenocorticism doesn't usually cause weight gain—it causes weight *redistribution*. That fact, and a potbellied appearance, just looks like weight gain. Less than half a percent of Cushing's dogs actually have obesity (E. C. Feldman 1995).

- Enlarged liver (hepatomegaly) (51-67%). The enlarged liver can be detected by your vet upon examination. But to the average dog owner, it (along with the weight redistribution to the belly) just looks like a fat belly.

- Eating too much (polyphagia) (46-57%). If you find yourself feeding your pet more than usual, that ravenous appetite may not simply be a case of an overweight dog eating too much food.

- Muscle weakness (14-57%). You may notice your pet struggling to stand, swaying while walking, or they may trip over themselves.

- Muscle loss (muscle atrophy) (35%)Panting (30%). This may be accompanied by a collapsing trachea (breathing tube), especially common in small breeds (E. C. Feldman 1995). This is hard for an owner to detect, but your veterinarian will be able to diagnose a collapsing trachea with an ultrasound.

- Darkening hair color. Black coated dogs with Cushing's will often have a brownish or rust colored coat (Hines 2009).

Other, less frequent symptoms are:

- Lack of females being "in heat" (anestrus).

- In males, testicular atrophy (small, sponge-like testicles).

- Calcium deposits in the skin (calcinosis cutis). This is a textbook symptom which is rarely, if ever seen (Hines 2009).

- Facial nerve paralysis.

- Stiff gait and muscular problems (rare). This particular symptom has only been noted in 5 out of 800 dogs diagnosed with Cushing's in the literature. Your pet may limp, or may even be unable to move their back legs. Your vet will find muscle stiffness upon examination (E. C. Feldman 1995).

- Thromboembolism (the formation of blood clots deep inside the body's veins) has also been noted as a problem with Cushing's disease (E. C. Feldman 1995), as has thin or fragile skin, due to excess cortisone which causes the skin to get easily scraped and acquire infections. (E. C. Feldman 1995).

As an owner, you may also notice reduced activity due to a combination of the above problems. Your pet's sky high cortisone levels cause the leg muscles to atrophy and their liver to enlarge (Hines 2009). It's no wonder your dog doesn't feel up to their usual level of exercise and activities. Your pet may not feel like their usual walks, they may sleep a lot, or they may be lethargic and depressed.

These symptoms can be characteristic of a slew of disease, and not just Cushing's disease. In fact, a veterinarian cannot diagnose Cushing's disease based on appearances and anecdotal evidence alone. Only laboratory tests can say for certain if your dog has hypercorticolism.

Chapter Four: Diagnosis

Many tests can tell a veterinarian if your dog has Cushing's disease and what the causes of the hormonal imbalance are. However, these tests aren't 100% foolproof. Probst (1998) describes how a veterinarian, Dr. Charles Wiedmeyer, researched ways veterinarians could improve their diagnostic capabilities. "Initially, you can look at an animal and suspect Cushing's disease," Wiedmeyer says, "but obtaining a definitive diagnosis can be a challenge."

There are many tests that can be used to aid in a diagnosis Cushing's disease. A routine blood analysis of a dog with Cushing's disease will often show higher than normal levels of Alkaline Phosphatase (ALP), Alanine aminotransferase (ALT), cholesterol and blood glucose in addition to very dilute urine. Further tests can identify if the problem is in the pituitary gland or the adrenal glands, and ultrasound examination can be used to detect tumors. None of these tests give a definitive diagnosis: further tests are necessary. One such test is a dexamethasone suppression test, widely considered to be the most accurate diagnostic tool currently available.

The Urine Cortisol:Creatinine Ratio (UC:Cr)

This is a urine test where your veterinarian will obtain a urine sample and compare the ratios of cortisol and creatinine in the urine.

A negative test on this test will rule out Cushing's disease, while a positive result (a high ratio) will warrant further tests. This is because a variety of disorders can cause the same high ratio, including liver, intestinal, kidney, heart and autoimmune disease) (Brooks, Testing: Confirming Cushing's Syndrome 2006).

Low Dose Dexamethasone Suppression Test

When dexamethasone is administered to your pet, their pituitary gland will detect the dexamethasone and signal the adrenal glands to stop producing cortisol. The typical response seen in a normal dog is a drop in cortisol level about eight hours after the dexamethasone is administered. In a dog with a pituitary tumor, the dexamethasone has no effect (the pituitary continues to signal the adrenals to continue production of cortisol), and there is no change is cortisol levels at the end of the eight hour period. This procedure requires an eight hour stay in the hospital (Brooks, Testing: Confirming Cushing's Syndrome 2006). However, a negative result on this test does not mean that your dog doesn't have Cushing's disease—it just means that they most likely to not have a pituitary tumor, which is the most common form of Cushing's disease.

ACTH Stimulation Test

The ACTH is the only test that can diagnose Iatrogenic (veterinarian-induced) Cushing's disease. Adrenocorticotrophic hormone (ACTH) is the hormone that the pituitary gland releases to signal the adrenal glands to produce cortisol. Your veterinarian will administer a dose of ACTH to your dog. If a rise in cortisol levels is found, it may indicate Cushing's disease. The test should take about two hours, although your dog will have to have fasted the night before. The ACTH stimulation test may also be used by your vet to monitor your dog's progress after a diagnosis of Cushing's. A downside is that the test is time consuming and expensive.

Adrenal Tumors

If tests indicate your dog has an adrenal cortical tumor, surgery to remove the tumor is one option, if it hasn't spread to other parts of your pet's body. Unfortunately, in about 50% of cases, the tumor is malignant and may have already spread. Surgery may, in those cases, not be an option (Hahn 1997). Even if your pet is suited for surgery, it's a fairly high risk operation: in one study by E.C. Feldman (1995), 63 out of 102 dogs with adrenal tumors were given the okay for surgery. Out of those 63 dogs, two thirds had successful surgeries. Four had "an inoperable mass" and were euthanized, and 18 died from surgical complications. If your pet survives the surgery, you can expect them to live, on average, about four years after the procedure. Feldman goes on to describe how removal of the adrenal glands in advanced cases is a possibility, but because of the high risk surgery (your dog's immune system is already taking a beating) and ready availability of drugs, the risks associated with surgery may in some cases be too high. Each case is different: make sure you talk with your vet about your pet's particular circumstance, and the risks involved with the procedure.

Pituitary Dependent

Surgery for pituitary dependent tumors is rare. Removal of the pituitary gland has been performed on dogs in the past, but the procedure is considered by most veterinarians to be too risky (E. C. Feldman 1995). Because there are now many drugs available to treat pituitary dependent tumors, in most cases the risks of surgery are unwarranted. In December 2008, the Food and Drug Administration (FDA) approved the first drug in over a decade (Trilostane) for Cushing's disease in dogs. There are currently four medications for *pituitary dependent Cushing's disease:*

1. Trilostane (Vetoryl®)
2. L-Deprenyl hydrochloride (Anipryl®, Eldepryl® Carbex®, or selegiline)
3. Mitotane or o,p'-DDD (Lysodren®)
4. Ketoconazole (Nizoral®)

Trilostane

Trilostane is the only FDA approved drug that can treat pituitary *and* adrenal-dependent Cushing's disease in dogs. The drug works by stopping cortisol production in the adrenals. Trilostane works by stopping the action of an enzyme called 3-beta-hydroxysteroid dehydrogenase, which is involved in cortisol production. The medication is taken once or twice a day with food.

According to the FDA (2009), your pet should not be medicated with trilostane if they:

- have kidney or liver disease

- takes certain heart disease medication

- are pregnant

Side effects may include:

- vomiting

- mild lethargy (lack of energy)

- diarrhea

- weight loss

- Addisonian reactions (your dog may show signs of Addison's disease—the opposite of Cushing's). These life-threatening or permanent reactions can occur at any dose, and are unpredictable. The risk is about 2-3% ((Brooks, Treatment: Pituitary Cushing's Syndrome 2001).

L-Deprenyl hydrochloride (Anipryl®, Eldepryl® Carbex®, or selegiline)

Anipryl (selegiline) is FDA-approved for the treatment of uncomplicated, pituitary-dependent Cushing's disease in dogs. The drug, originally designed to treat Parkinson's disease in humans, was discovered as a treatment for Cushing's disease in dogs during animal testing for Parkinson's disease. When researchers were experimenting on the animals with the drug, they discovered that the dogs' ACTH production was shutting down. An important piece of information for you to consider when deciding if L-Deprenyl is right for your dog is the following fact: while the manufacturer's initial claim was that 80% of dogs see an improvement on L-Deprenyl, independent studies show that only 20% of dogs improve while on the drug (Brooks, Treatment: Pituitary Cushing's Syndrome 2001).

The drug works by directly suppressing the pituitary gland's action. In addition, L-Deprenyl is a monoamine oxidase inhibitor which works on brain chemistry and stops ACTH production in part by encouraging the production of dopamine, itself an ACTH inhibitor. When dopamine levels are high, ACTH production stops (Mar Vista Animal Medical Center U.D.). The part of the pituitary gland where dopamine is active is called the pars intermedia. About 20% of pituitary dependent Cushing's disease cases will have a tumor in this particular area—the drug will not have any effect if the tumor is in a different spot. (Brooks, L-Deprenyl Hydrochloride (Anipryl, Eldepryl, Carbex) January).

Side effects of L-Deprenyl include:

- Diarrhea
- Disorientation
- Drooling
- Hearing loss
- Itchy skin
- Listlessness
- Loss of appetite

- Nausea
- Restlessness
- Tremors
- Vomiting

Side effects occur in about 5% of cases (Brooks, Treatment: Pituitary Cushing's Syndrome 2001).

Monitoring with L-Deprenyl can present a challenge, mostly because the regular monitoring tests (like the ACTH stim) can't assist with detecting L-Deprenyl's action on the brain.

Contraindications

Do not use L-Deprenyl with:

- The parasite control Amitraz (Mitaban dips, Preventic tick collars, or Promeris).
- The psychoactive drugs Fluoxetine (discontinue use 5 weeks prior to starting L-Deprenyl), mirtazapine, amitriptyline, and clomipramine.
- The urinary incontinence drug phenylpropanolamine (discontinue at least 2 weeks before starting L-Deprenyl.
- Narcotics such as meperidine.

(Brooks, Treatment: Pituitary Cushing's Syndrome 2001)

Mitotane or o,p'-DDD (Lysodren®)

Lysodren is a human chemotherapy drug that has shown to be useful in treating Cushing's disease in dogs since 1973 (E. C. Feldman 1995). Although not technically indicated for the treatment of Cushing's, many veterinarians use the drug "off label," meaning that they prescribe a drug for something other than it is approved by the DFA for. Mitotane is a derivative of the pesticide DDT and works by destroying the parts of the adrenal glands that produce cortisol (Hahn 1997).

Veterinarian Dr. Wiedmeyer (as cited in Probst, 1998) states that "You have to monitor the disease very closely because you are wiping out part of the adrenal gland in the process." Dr. Wiedmeyer continues by saying that essentially, Lysodren works by killing the cortisol producing glands. Although it is an inexpensive treatment, careful monitoring is essential—the side effects can be severe. Side effects include:

- Addison's Disease (where not enough cortisol is produced). See Appendix A for a full description of Addison's disease.

- Loss of appetite

- Nausea

- Vomiting

- Diarrhea

The odds of your pet having at least one of these side effects is around 30% (Brooks, Treatment: Pituitary Cushing's Syndrome 2001).

The risk of permanent Addison's disease is one reason why Lysodren is no longer the Cushing's disease drug of choice for many veterinarians.

When your veterinarian prescribes Lysodren, they will also give you an antidote pill, should an Addisonian reaction occur. Your veterinarian may recommend a decrease in food intake, because it's best if your dog is hungry during the first few days of treatment (remember, Cushing's disease dogs often have a ravenous appetite). You'll need to return to your vet for an ATCH test once your dog shows signs of not being so hungry (for example, they may not finish all of their food). During treatment, you should contact your vet immediately if you notice any of the following symptoms:

- Diarrhea or vomiting

- Appetite loss (even mild to moderate)

- Decrease in thirst

- Tiredness or listlessness

This does not necessarily indicate there is a problem—it may indicate a need for an antidote pill or it may be a sign the treatment is working and that it's time for an ACTH test. Your veterinarian will be the best person to advise you about the best option at this point.

The risk of relapse with Lysodren is high, about 50%, and it may take many months for symptoms of Cushing's to disappear completely. Approximately half of dogs undergoing treatment will relapse at some point and require another round of induction.

Ketoconazole (Nizoral®)

Ketoconazole was first developed to treat fungal infections in humans. Although eventually found to be unsuitable as a fungal infection drug because of hormonal side effects, it became widely used for the treatment of Cushing's disease in dogs in the 1990s where it was found about 80% of dogs improved while on the drug (Brooks, Treatment: Pituitary Cushing's Syndrome 2001). It is not a tremendously popular drug, perhaps in part because it is very expensive when compared to other treatment options.

Side effects include:

- Vomiting

- Diarrhea

Treatment for Iatrogenic Cushing's

Iatrogenic Cushing's is caused by medications (such as some medications given for skin infections or even Addison's disease). The treatment is a slow withdrawal from the offending drug with your veterinarians help. It is not advisable to discontinue use suddenly, because of the risk of serious (and potentially fatal) withdrawal effects (Hahn 1997).

"Treating Cushing's is a balancing act," Dr. Stohlman says on the FDA website. "But dogs with the disease can live a good life if they are monitored closely by a veterinarian and the owner is diligent about bringing the dog in for blood work and giving the medication as directed."

Chapter Six: Associated Medical Complications

An excess of steroids (such as the ones used to treat Cushing's disease) over the long run can have a detrimental effect on a dog's overall health (E. C. Feldman 1995).

Hypertension

Hypertension is an extremely common problem in Cushing's patients. The complication may lead to a host of secondary disorders including blindness, heart failure, and problems with the kidney which may in turn lead to blood clotting problems. According to Feldman (1995), hypertension can be found in over 50% of Cushing's syndrome dogs. "Normal dogs," Feldman states, "have systolic, diastolic, and mean blood pressure of about 150, 90, and 100 mmHg respectively. Dogs with Cushing's have systolic, diastolic, and mean blood pressures of 180, 120, and 145 mmHg, respectively."

Pyelonephritis and Urinary Calculi

Cushing's disease dogs are predisposed to urinary tract infections. You want to make sure this infection doesn't reach the kidneys causing a kidney infection (pyelonephritis), where it can cause severe complications. A small percentage (under ten percent) of Cushing's disease dogs have urinary calcium formations (calculi) because of increased calcium excretion (E. C. Feldman 1995).

Diabetes Mellitus

1 in 10 dogs with Cushing's disease will develop diabetes mellitus (Center 2010). Watch for a marked increase in thirst or urine output, which could be a sign of the disease. Your vet can also test for an increase of glucose in your pet's urine (E. C. Feldman 1995).

If your dog develops diabetes, they will have to be treated for both diabetes mellitus *and* hyperadrenocorticism and will likely require large doses of insulin.

Managing this dual condition can be quite the challenge for the dog owner, although about 5-10% of dual-diagnosed dogs won't require insulin once their Cushing's disease has been stabilized (E. C. Feldman 1995). Hypophysectomy (surgical removal of the pituitary gland) has just recently been shown to be an effective treatment to resolve diabetes in a Cushing's disease dog (Ishino H 2009).

Pulmonary Thromboembolism

Cushing's disease dogs are more likely to have problems with blood clots.

Chapter Seven: Feeding your Cushing's Dog a Natural Diet

Cushing's dogs have a compromised immune system; it goes without saying that you should feed your pet the most nutritious ingredients available. By providing your dog with a home-made diet, you'll avoid some of the shocking ingredients found in commercial food, including euthanized animals.

After reading the book <u>Food Pets Die For: Shocking Facts About Pet Food</u> by Ann Martin and finding out that the "premium" commercial dog food I was feeding my dog may have contained rancid and moldy food products, toxic chemicals, diseased cattle and euthanized animals, I decided to research a little further. The statements are very much true, and have been acknowledged by the FDA, who found pentobarbital, a substance used to euthanize animals, in dog food.

These products were found to contain pentobarbital:

- Pro Plan Beef and Rice Puppy
- Nutro Premium
- Ol'Roy Krunchy Bites & Bones
- Ol"Roy Premium Formula with Chicken
- Ol'Roy High Performance with Chicken
- Ol'Roy Meaty Chunks
- Ol'Roy Puppy formula
- Ol'Roy Lean

- Trailblazer Chunk Premium Quality
- Trailblazer Bite Size Ration
- Dad's Bite Size Meal
- Weis Value Chunky and Moist
- Weis Value Puppy Food
- Weis Value Crunchy
- Weis Value Gravy Style
- Weis Total High Energy
- Super G Chunk Style
- Rich Food Chunk Style
- Rich Food Gravy Style
- Rich Food High Protein
- Pet Essentials Chunk Style
- America's Choice Krunchy Kibble
- Ken-L-Ration Gravy Train
- Heinz Kibbles and Bits Jerky, Puppy, Lean, Beefy
- Champ Chunx Bite Size
- Kibble Select Premium
- Pet Gold Master Puppy

Note that the FDA didn't test every dog food. In fact, they just took samples from one store. So just because your brand isn't on there does not mean it doesn't have euthanized animals in it!

You can try a vegetarian dog food for your Cushing's disease dog, like Nature's Recipe Vegetarian Dog Food, which provides complete nutrition. It's the only vegetarian product recommended by R.M. Clemmons, DVM, PhD, Associate Professor of Neurology & Neurosurgery for the Department of Small Animal Clinical Sciences at the University of Florida, who specializes in the nutrition of immune compromised dogs, such as those dogs with Cushing's disease. You'll be guaranteed of no euthanized animals in your pet's bowl. But that may not rule out moldy grain and other nasty by-products.

If you want to feed your pet a more natural diet, Dr. Clemmons recommends the following complete diet for dogs:

- Basic diet: (1 serving size equals 1 can of commercial food, provides 1160-1460 calories per serving, and feeds a dog approximately 30-50 pounds)
- Boiled, baked, or fried (olive oil), chicken (2oz)
- Tofu (4oz)
- Long Grain Brown Rice (3 oz, prepared in 6 oz water)
- Extra Virgin Olive Oil (2 oz)
- Molasses (Â¼ cup)
- Boiled and cut up Carrots (2)
- Cooked Spinach (1 cup)
- Chopped and Steamed Green Bell Pepper (4 Tbs)
- Boiled and Chopped Broccoli Spears (4)

The above ingredients can be frozen for up to one month, and defrosted before serving. Before serving, add:

- Dry Ground Ginger (1 tsp.)
- Crushed Raw Garlic Cloves (2)
- Dry Mustard (Â½ tsp)
- Bone Meal (1 tsp)

Dr. Clemmons recommends that you weigh your dog while following this diet, and feed more or less each week depending on whether your dog is losing weight or gaining weight. Make sure to introduce the new food gradually into your dog's diet.

Tofu, Dr. Clemmons states, is full of flavenoids and other ingredients to promote overall health. Garlic and ginger are natural anti-inflammatory substances, antibiotics, and anti-fungal agents. Ginger also calms the stomach. Mustard improves digestion and bowel function.

Chapter Eight: Genetics and Inheritability

Genetics is a major cause of Cushing's disease in dogs. According to Dr. Anita Oberbauer—professor at the University of California, Davis Department of Animal Science—dogs are "the most genetically engineered species on the planet" due to a long history of breeding dogs for desirable traits and breeding out undesirable characteristics (Oberbauer 01-JAN-2006).

Many years ago, when I was living in the United Kingdom, I bred working Siberian Huskies. I had a basic understanding of genetics—enough to know that when I wanted to breed all-white Siberians into my line, that I had to find a sire and a dam with the recessive and elusive white gene and breed them together. A few months later, my bitch produced a litter of six puppies: three grey and white, two black and white, and one white. This was a result of a little knowledge, and a lot of good luck. Why "luck"? Choosing a sire and dam that carry those traits was nothing more than an educated guess; it isn't possible to tell what genes a dog has just by looking at it. A dog breeder must look at pedigrees and use the laws of probability to breed a trait in, or breed one out.

Not being able to "see" genes are part of the reason why it's difficult to breed out Cushing's disease from an affected population. You can't tell what dogs are carriers for the disease by looking at them, and there's no DNA test (at time of writing) that will tell you which dogs are carriers. However, a basic understanding of genetics and probabilities could prevent a lot of heartache in the future. At a minimum, sires and dams who have produced litters of Cushing's pups should not be bred from again unless the breeder is certain which parent has the gene for the disease.

How inheritability works

Every cell in the body contains DNA, or deoxyribonucleic acid. DNA is made up of repeating pieces of information located on nucleotide bases. The sections of DNA that give instructions on how to make and operate a living organism are called *genes*. The genes are located in compacted sections of DNA called *chromosomes*. Dogs have over 20,000 genes and 38 pairs of chromosomes in each cell (Oberbauer & Bell, n.d.).

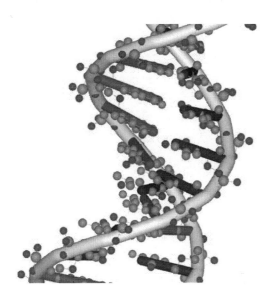

Double helix DNA structure. One section of DNA, like the one depicted here, can be thought of as a gene.

Each pair of non-sex chromosomes is called an *autosome*. Because autosomes come in pairs, each gene has two possible states, called *alleles*. Alleles can be identical (homozygous) or different (heterozygous).

The chromosome(s) responsible for diseases are always found at the same location —for example in Portuguese water dogs, the loci associated with late onset Addison's disease is always chromosomes CFA12 and 37 (Chase K 2006).

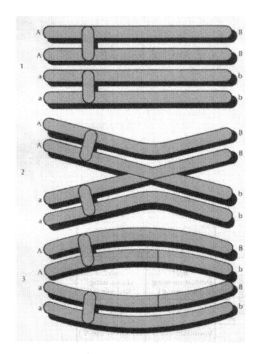

A model of chromosomes.

When a hereditary trait is referred to as *dominant*, it means that if an allele has a certain characteristic (i.e. short legs), it will show up no matter what the other paired allele is coded for. According to Adam Miklósi, author of the book Dog Behavior, evolution and cognition, short legs in dogs is actually a genetic abnormality called achondroplasia, where the legs stop growing during puppyhood. Because short legs are a dominant trait (like brown eyes in humans), a long-legged dog and a short-legged dog can be bred together to result in a short-legged dog every time. By mating dogs together in this way, the abnormality becomes "fixed" in certain dog populations. This resulted in the dachshunds and Chihuahuas of today.

On the other hand, a *recessive* trait means that in order for the trait to appear, two alleles must be exactly the same. An example of a recessive trait is blue eyes in Siberian huskies—in order for the trait to show through, both alleles must carry the chromosome for blue eye color.

A third type of trait is also possible, called incomplete dominance, where the trait may or may not show through. For example, spots on a dog's coat is an example of incomplete dominance. A dog many have heavy spotting, no spotting, or if they are a heterozygous individual (i.e. one allele is dominant and the other is recessive), they might have mild spotting.

The heritability of a trait is designated with a number from 0 to 1. The designation '0' means that there is no probability of inheriting the trait for a population and that the trait is entirely environmental. Spoken language in humans is an example of a trait that is environmental (heritability=0) as is a cropped tail in dogs (for the uninitiated, tail docking is performed by people—it is not inherited).[1] A designation of 1 means that there is 100% certainty the trait will show up if the affected allele is present in a population. Blood type is an example of a trait that is inherited (heritability=1). Dr. Anita Oberbauer (2006) reports that for Portuguese Water Dogs, Addison's disease has an inheritability of 0.49 (+/- 0.16). Dr. Oberbauer's research also suggests that Addison's is most likely due

---

[1] Dogs' tail docking has actually been banned in the UK since 2007 by the Animal Welfare Act.

to a recessive mode of inheritance (i.e. two identical alleles are needed for the disease to manifest) and the more inbred an animal is, the higher the likelihood of Addison's; highly inbred dogs in the study had up to a 25% chance of being affected with Addison's disease. Research is continuing in many breeds under CGAP as Dr. Oberbauer's team continues to work on discovering the location of the affected genes on the chromosomes.

However, considering that Cushing's disease is more prevalent in the genetically engineered dog population than in the more diverse human population, it stands to reason that there are genes responsible for Cushing's disease and eventually those genes will be identified, enabling dog breeders to take steps to eradicate the inheritability of the disease in dogs.

Chapter Nine: Do Vaccinations cause Cushing's Disease?

Some schools of thought have suggested vaccinations may trigger immune system disorders (uval D 1996). [2] Most of us visit the veterinarian once a year with Fluffy or Rover for yearly vaccinations, thinking that we are responsible pet owners for remembering that yearly visit. I never gave this annual event a second thought until my dog developed Addison's disease and I conducted some research into the possible causes. I discovered that vaccines are thought in some circles to cause immune disorders in dogs, so I'll be foregoing her usual annual shots in favor of titer tests.

Shortly after Shakti was diagnosed with Addison's, a post on an Addison's discussion forum caught my eye: a woman who said her poodle, "Timmy", came down with Addison's disease two and a half weeks after he received his annual booster shots. This came at the time when Shakti was due for her annual booster—four months after her initial Addison's diagnosis. I decided to look into vaccinations before I took Shakti for her yearly check up. I was shocked to learn that these annual visits aren't actually recommended by any major

---

[2] Duval and Giger's study showed 15 of 58 dogs at the Veterinary Hospital of the University of Pennsylvania over a 27 month period developed idiopathic IMHA (immune-mediated hemolytic anaemia) within one month after vaccinations.

organization or drug manufacturer and may actually be harming our dogs.[3]

Most dogs are vaccinated annually against distemper, leptospirosis, canine adenovirus-1 and hepatitis, canine parainfluenza virus, canine parvovirus, canine Corona virus as well as canine bordatella (kennel cough) and Lyme disease. Vaccines work by stimulating the immune system to produce antibodies to a particular disease; if the dog is exposed at a later date to the pathogen, antibodies will attack and neutralize the disease.

The "puppy shots" (those vaccinations given in puppyhood), are recommended by most veterinarians. It's the adult booster shots that are causing the most controversy. Until recently, vaccine manufacturers recommended that all dogs be given a booster shot once a year. Veterinarians were in agreement—yearly booster shots are a way to encourage animal owners to visit every year and increase income. However, in 2003, the American Animal Hospital Association (AAHA) released new guidelines and recommendations for shots that differed from the once a year visit that most pet owners were used to.

The AAHA designated four core vaccines that are necessary because of the serious nature of the pathogens: distemper,

---

[3] I have excluded rabies from this discussion: most states require regular rabies shots once a year—consult your local animal control department for details.

parvovirus, adenovirus-2, and rabies. For distemper, parvovirus, and adenovirus-2, the recommendations are:

- Vaccinate at 6-8 weeks, 9-11 weeks, and 12-14 weeks.
- Give a booster shot at one year old.
- Subsequent booster shots should be administered every three years unless indicated otherwise (i.e. dogs at high risk may need more frequent shots and owners of dogs with immune disorders may want to forego shots for their pets in favor of titer tests).

There are many factors that an owner needs to take into consideration when deciding how often to vaccinate (and which diseases to vaccinate against), including:

- Reported duration of immunity from each shot (not all drugs are created equal; shots from different manufacturers will have different durations).
- Health and lifestyle of each pet (i.e. indoor vs. outdoor).
- Probability of contracting any particular disease (i.e. working dogs are exposed to more infectious agents than family pets). Dogs that roam, who have contact with wild animals or swim in streams are all at higher risk from contracting disease.
- Public health concerns (i.e. rabies shots are required frequently by law).

Pfizer, one of the major manufacturers of dog vaccines, reported in a study published in the Journal of American Veterinary

Medicine in January 2004 that vaccines can protect a dog for four years or more, giving credence to the new guidelines issues by the AAHA. Other studies have found that immunity can last up to seven years.

As Shakti definitely falls into the category of "immune-compromised," I chose to forego her annual shots from now on. Additionally, she's at low risk for most diseases: she stays at home when we are away (we have a pet sitter), and she rarely plays with other dogs—even at the dog park, she keeps to herself. Every couple of years I'll get a titer test done to make sure she is fully immunized against the major diseases.

When the time comes to revaccinate (which I hope we can put off for many years, perhaps even a lifetime), I'll weigh the risk of possible side effects with the risk of her contracting a life-threatening illness. If she does need a shot, I'll ask my vet to get a vaccine from a company that does not put additives into their shots: Intervet is one such company, another is Heska, which produces intranasal vaccines.

Titer Testing—an alternative to vaccines

Titer tests measure how much antibody to a certain pathogen is in your dog's system at the time of the test. Several titer tests are available on the market: your veterinarian may have them or you may need to ask your vet to special order them. Titer tests are available for major diseases like distemper and parvovirus. There's also a rabies titer test available but this does not substitute for proof of rabies protection—you must still comply with local laws and have your dog vaccinated even if they have a positive titer test. Research has shown that up to 95.1% of dogs were protected against parvovirus one to two years after their last vaccinations (Twark L 2000). However, titer tests are not a perfect alternative and come with their own set of issues including false negatives (Moore January 15, 2004, Vol. 224, No. 2,).[4]

After your pet's blood is drawn, the lab will dilute the blood sample. If the blood is diluted 1,000 times and antibodies are still present, your pet's ratio would show up as 1:1000 on the test form. For parvovirus, a protective titer should be above 1:80 and for distemper, above 1:96 is considered protective. If your dog has a value higher than these figures, it means that your dog does not need a booster shot. The lab will record your pet's titer as "low" or "high" along with the ratio.

At first, a titer test seems like a good alternative to re-vaccinating: if your dog's titer shows high antibodies—great! If

---

[4] Researchers Morre & Glickman (2004) state that in a hypothetical group of 1,000 dogs tested, 86 might have false negative titers. Still, 86 dogs vaccinated unnecessarily might be better than all 1,000 being revaccinated, which is what would happen without the availability of a titer test.

antibodies are low, then it would seem a good time to vaccinate. However, titer tests don't work quite that simply, and a low titer could cause you to give an unnecessary booster shot.

A 2002 report from the American Veterinary Medical Association did state that titer testing is, for the most part, unreliable. However, many others advocate titer tests as a guide to determine whether you should vaccinate your pet. If you are considering a titer blood test in lieu of vaccinating, the ultimate decision is up to you— but in an immune compromised dog with Addison's disease, a titer test just might be the right choice.

Chapter Ten: Cheaper Treatment Options

If your dog has Cushing's disease, canine Addison's disease, or a dual diagnosis of Cushing's and diabetes, you might experience sticker shock at the veterinary office. A month's supply of replacement hormones could cost over two hundred dollars a month for a large dog. However, it is possible to reduce the cost of treatment, or even get it for free!

Shop Around for drugs

At her diagnosis for Addison's disease, our border collie, Shakti, weighed 33 lbs. One shot of Percorten-V (1.33ml) cost $69 at the veterinarian. On top of that, we had to pay $15 for prednisone every 20 days. Money was tight at the time—so I did a little shopping around and reduced our monthly cost from $80 to $55 for all medicines.

1. **Google is your friend**, but don't expect miracles: The cheapest price for a 4ml bottle of Percorten-V I found on the internet at time of writing was $150 ("on sale"). I followed one ad for $138.50 to a generic pet .com website but when I got there—surprise, surprise the price had jumped to $179.99. Even if I could get a vial of Percorten-V at $138.50, that's still $46.16 per

dose...and you have to buy the needles and administer it yourself on top of that.

2. Try **compounding pharmacies** for cheap medications. Here are a few to consider:

Nora Apothecary (www.noraapothecary.com)

1 (800) 729-0276

Congaree Veterinary Pharmacy (www.congareevetrx.com)

1 (877) 939-1335

Valley Drug and Compounding (www.1pharmacy.com)

1 (818) 788-0635

Pet Pharm (www.petpharm.org)

Summit Chemist (www.svprx.ca) (in Canada)

1-866-794-7387

3. **Find the cheapest vet around and give him your business:** There's a well-known pet clinic in my home town called Herschel Animal clinic. They don't have the bells and whistles of the upscale veterinary practices (they rarely answer their phone and there's no brightly lit, cushy waiting room—sometimes you have to wait out in the parking lot for an hour or two to be seen). But they are cheap, and for someone with a dog with a chronic disease, that can literally be a lifesaver. We're charged only $45 per 1.33ml shot of Percorten-V and a month's supply of

prednisone is $10. Shakti and I take a book, a bone, and a Starbucks, and just enjoy the time together while we wait.

4. Cut down on the dosage of medications **with your vet's help**: tell your vet that you would like to decrease your pet's medication. Your vet will check your pet's electrolytes every month for a few months until you've reached the lowest maintenance dose possible. Initially, this will be expensive, say $50 per month for the additional blood work for 6 months. But it might save you $20-30 a month thereafter in decreased medications.

Finally, if you can't afford it, find a way to afford it: one reason that Dr. Plant at Herschel offers medications at the lowest price possible is because he knows they are sometimes prohibitively expensive. One former client of his just didn't get the treatment for their dog, and the animal "just wasted away," he said. "It was sad, sad." The fact is, your dog must have replacement hormones, or they will die. Although there isn't a free pet clinic system in the states like there is in the UK (the PSDA), there are many routes you can try to obtain reduced cost, or even free, care.

• **Write a letter to your vet:** this will probably work if you've been a long term client and are likely to continue being a client in the future. Write a personal letter and tell him that you cannot afford full treatment costs. Tell him what you *can* afford a month. Ask him/her for their help. Remember that your vet will still have to purchase the drug at base, so don't expect miracles. But it's worth a shot (if you'll excuse the pun).

- **Contact shelters and rescue organizations in your area** and ask them if they know of any low cost clinics. One website— www.pets911.com, offers a search feature where you can enter your zip code and find local rescue and animal organizations that may be able to help.

- **Consider finding another home for your pet.** If you have a purebred animal, contact your nearest breed-specific rescue and tell them that you are having trouble affording medications. Some rescue organizations will allow you to advertise for a new home on their website, and someone who is familiar with Cushing's might be willing to give your dog a home. You can also look for breed-specific rescue discussion boards—there are many on the web. Whatever you do, make sure that you don't give your animal to the local animal control or city-run shelter; they immediately euthanize sick animals.

- **Make A Wish:** if all else fails you can try posting for help on the Make a Wish page at www.wishuponahero.com. They match donors to people with needs. You never know when an angel (maybe a local vet?) will offer a helping hand!

Appendix A: What is an Addisonian Crisis?

Symptoms of Addison's disease can be so nonspecific that they are commonly attributed to other diseases. That's why it's so important to take your dog to the vet when they are ill–something as simple as an upset stomach could be something much more serious.

Dogs with Addison's disease might at first appear to have a gastrointestinal disease–they might be vomiting, have diarrhea and a poor appetite. You might also notice that they drink more frequently and urinate more often. The signs may be so subtle that you don't notice any signs at all–that is until they have an Addisonian crisis and collapse. A dog can go from being fine to having an Addisonian crisis in just a few hours.

An Addisonian crisis is a medical emergency. Symptoms can be vague and mimic gastrointestinal disorders, acute renal failure, liver disease, insulinoma, hypothyroidism or hypoglycemia. Here are the symptoms that are generally indicative of an Addisonian crisis:

- lethargy
- slow heart rate (bradycardia)
- not eating
- drinking and urinating frequently
- severe weakness
- vomiting blood (rare)

- blood in the stool (rare)
- seizures due to hypoglycemia (rare)

Also known as hypoadrenocorticism, adrenal insufficiency, or hypocortisolism. Addison's disease occurs when the adrenal glands—located above the kidneys—fail to produce enough hormones to keep the body functioning normally. This includes the hormone cortisol.

You should be aware of the symptoms of Addison's disease—it could strike any dog, at any time and without prompt medical attention your pet could be dead within hours if not treated with emergency medical care. In some cases (such as too much Lysodren), your vet may tell you to administer an antidote pill, which should reverse the Addisonian reaction in about 30 minutes (Brooks, Treatment: Pituitary Cushing's Syndrome 2001).

Appendix B: Definitions

Adrenocorticotropic hormone (ACTH) stimulation test: This test signals the adrenal glands to produce cortisol. If the adrenal glands are working normally, cortisol levels should rise.

Addisonian crisis: a medical emergency involving several factors including shock, cardiovascular collapse, atrial standstill, low blood volume and electrolyte disturbances.

Adrenal cortex: part of the adrenal glands that secrete glucocorticoids like cortisol and mineralocorticoids like aldosterone.

Adrenal Glands: Part of the body responsible for regulation of stress hormones that lies behind the kidneys. Consists of two parts: inner medulla and outer cortex. The adrenal cortex secretes glucocorticoids like cortisol and mineralocorticoids like aldosterone.

Aldosterone: a corticosteroid hormone secreted by the adrenal cortex which regulates salt and water balance in the body

Atrial standstill: a heart arrhythmia caused by electrolyte imbalances, particularly high potassium levels. Can be reversed in Addison's by rapid infusion of IV fluids.

Atypical Addison's disease: where only the cortisol producing part of the adrenal cortex isn't working *or* Addison's dogs who present without the classic electrolyte changes (i.e. low sodium and high potassium) seen in primary Addison's.

Azotemia: elevated kidney parameters, i.e. high urea in the blood as shown by the serum BUN (blood urea nitrogen) level test.

Bradycardia: slow heart rate.

BUN (blood urea nitrogen) level test: used to detect elevated kidney parameters.

Calcium gluconate: a mineral supplement usually used to correct low levels of calcium in the blood (hypocalcemia) and heart arrhythmias.

Capillary Refill Time: the time is takes for blood to refill empty capillaries. Normal capillary refill time in a healthy dog is 1 second.

Cortisol: a glucocorticoid hormone secreted by the adrenal cortex that regulates blood sugar.

Cardiovascular collapse: sudden failure of the heart to produce output.

Corticosteroid: a class of hormones produced by the adrenal glands that includes glucocorticoids and mineralcorticoids.

Cortisol: a stress-fighting glucocorticoid produced by the adrenal gland.

Edema: swelling causes by excessive accumulation of water in the body.

Electrolytes: salts found in the blood such as sodium, potassium and calcium.

Florinef: a brand name glucocorticoid and mineralcorticoid replacement.

Glucocorticoid: hormones produced by the adrenal glands that affect multiple body systems including appetite stimulation, maintaining blood glucose levels and controlling water, calcium, and red/white blood cell levels in the blood.

Hematemesis: vomiting blood.

Hyperkalemia: elevated potassium level due to lack of the adrenal hormone aldosterone.

Hypernatremia: high levels of salt in the blood (an electrolyte imbalance).

Hypochloremia: an electrolyte disturbance characterized by low levels of chloride ions in the blood.

Hypocholesterolemia: low levels of cholesterol in the blood.

Hypocortisolism: low levels of cortisol in the blood.

Hypokalemia: low levels of potassium in the blood.

Hyponatremia: low levels of salt in the blood.

Hypoproteinemia: low level of protein in the blood.

Hypothyroidism: underproduction of hormones by the thyroid gland. Can lead to weight gain, dry skin, and constipation.

Hypovolemia: a decreased amount of blood circulating in the body.

Ketoconazole: a medication used to treat fungal infections.

Melena: dark, tarry stools (usually a product of blood in the stool).

Metabolic acidosis: overly acidic blood.

Mineralocorticoid: hormones secreted by the adrenal cortex that regulate salt and water balance in the body. Mineralcorticoid deficiency leads to high potassium levels, low salt levels, and poor heart function. Aldosterone has major mineralcorticoid activity in the body but cortisol also plays a minor part.

Percorten-V: a medication that replaces mineralcorticoids in the body.

Phagocytes: white blood cells (immune cells) that digest invading particles.

Pituitary gland: the gland at the base of the brain that is responsible for cortisol production. The pituitary gland produces adrenocorticotropic hormone (ACTH) which signals the adrenal glands to produce cortisol.

Polydipsia: excessive thirst.

Polyuria: excessive urination.

Potassium: a mineral that is essential for body function (an electrolyte).

Prednisolone: prednisone's active metabolite.

Prednisone: a corticosteroid replacement (otherwise referred to as cortisol replacement/stress hormone replacement). Usually given in combination with Percorten-V in primary Addison's or as a stand-alone drug in secondary Addison's.

Primary Addison's disease: the classic Addison's disease where the adrenal glands stop producing both mineralcorticoids and glucocorticoids.

Stress Leukogram: a characteristic white blood cell pattern that sick dogs normally exhibit as a result of cortisol release. Because Addison's dogs do not release cortisol, the absence of a stress leukogram in a blood panel is a hallmark for the disease.

Trichuriasis: whipworm. Causes similar symptoms to Addison's disease.

Typical Addison's disease: adrenal glands that are not producing both cortisol and aldosterone.

Bibliography

Behrend EN, Kennis R. "Atypical Cushing's Syndrome in Dogs: Arguments For and Against." *The Veterinary Clinics of North America Small Animal Practice*, 2010: Mar 40(2):285-296.

Brooks, Wendy C. "L-Deprenyl Hydrochloride (Anipryl, Eldepryl, Carbex)." *Veterinary Partner*. 1 2001, January. http://www.veterinarypartner.com/Content.plx?P=A&S=0&C=0&A=556 (accessed March 1, 2010).

—. "Testing: Confirming Cushing's Syndrome." *Veterinary Partner*. April 17, 2006. http://www.veterinarypartner.com/Content.plx?P=A&S=0&C=0&A=636 (accessed March 16, 2010).

—. "Treatment: Pituitary Cushing's Syndrome." *Veterinary Partner*. January 1, 2001. http://www.veterinarypartner.com/Content.plx?P=A&S=0&C=0&A=637 (accessed March 6, 2010).

Castillo V, Giacomini D, Páez-Pereda M, Stalla J, Labeur M, Theodoropoulou M, Holsboer F, Grossman AB, Stalla GK, Arzt E. "Retinoic acid as a novel medical therapy for Cushing's disease in dogs." *Endocrinology*, 2006: Sep;147(9):4438-44.

Center, Mar Vista Animal Medical. "http://www.marvistavet.com/html/body_cushing_symptoms.html." *Cushing Symptoms*. January 10, 2010. http://www.marvistavet.com/html/body_cushing_symptoms.html (accessed March 11, 2010).

Chase K, Sargan D, Miller K, Ostrander E, Lark K. "Understanding the genetics of autoimmune disease: two loci that regulate late onset Addison's disease in Portuguese Water Dogs." *Int J Immunogenet*, 2006: Jun;33(3) 179-84.

Feldman, E. C. "Hyperadrenocorticism." In *Textbook of Veterinary Internal Medicine*, by S.J. Ettinger and E.C. Feldman (eds.), 1538-1577. 1995.

Feldman, Edward C. & Nelson, Richard W. "Therapy of Concurrent Diabetes Mellitus and Cushing's Syndrome." In *Canine and Feline Endocrinology and Reproduction, 2nd Edition, ,* by Edward C. & Nelson, Richard W. Feldman. 1996.

Felman, Edward C. "Therapy of Concurrent Diabetes Mellitus and Cushing's Syndrome (with o,p'-DDD/Lysodren)." In *Canine and Feline Endocrinology and Reproduction, 2nd Edition, ,* by Edward C. Feldman and Richard W. Nelson (Eds.). 1996.

Hahn, Joseph. "Cushing's Disease Affects Dogs, Cats, as Well as People." *Illinois University: College of Veterinary Medicine.* March 17, 1997. http://vetmed.illinois.edu/petcolumns/showarticle.cfm?id=175 (accessed March 11, 2010).

Hess, RS. "Insulin Resistance in Dogs." *The Veterinary Clinics of North America Small Animal Practice*, 2010: 40(2):309-316.

Hines, Ron. "Treating Cushing's Disease in Your Dog." *2nd Chance Info.* 2009. http://www.2ndchance.info/cushings.htm (accessed March 6, 2010).

Ishino H, Hara Y, Teshima T, Tanaka S, Takekoshi S, Nezu Y, Harada Y, Yogo T, Sako T, Koyama H, Teramoto A, Osamura RY, Tagawa M. "Hypophysectomy for a Dog with Coexisting Cushing's Disease and Diabetes Mellitus." *The Journal of Veterinary Medical Science*, 2009.

Laurenson, Michelle. "CANINE HYPERADRENOCORTICISM." *Veterinary Medical and Surgical Group.* u.d. 2010. http://www.vmsg.com/files/Case_Report_Canine_Hyuperadrenocorticism_and_Pseudomyotonia.pdf (accessed March 17, 2010).

Mar Vista Animal Medical Center. "L-DEPRENYL HYDROCHLORIDE SELEGILINE HYDROCHLORIDE." *Mar Vista Vet.* U.D. 2010 (accessed March 6, 2010).

Moore, G, Glickman, L. "A perspective on vaccine guidelines and titer tests for dogs." *Journal of the American Veterinary Medical Association*, January 15, 2004, Vol. 224, No. 2, : Pages 200-203.

Oberbauer, A. "Genetic evaluation of Addison's disease in the Portuguese Water Dog." *BMC Vet Res*, 01-JAN-2006: 2: 15.

Probst, Sarah. "Definitive Diagnosis Can Be Difficult in Cushing'sDisease." *University of Illinois: College of Veterinary Medicine.* August 10, 1998. http://vetmed.illinois.edu/petcolumns/showarticle.cfm?id=108 (accessed March 6, 2010).

Ramsey, IK. "Trilostane in Dogs." *The Veterinary Clinics of North America Small Animal Practice*, 2010: Mar;40(2):269-283.

Soothsoft. *Soothsoft Comfort Technology.* 2006. http://www.chillow.com/ (accessed March 6, 2010).

Twark L, Dodds WJ. " Clinical use of serum parvovirus and distemper virus antibody titers for determining revaccination strategies in healthy dogs." *J Am Vet Med Assoc*, 2000: 217:1021–1024.

U.S. Food and Drug Administration (FDA). "Treating Cushing's Disease in Dogs." *U.S. Food and Drug Administration.* August 3, 2009. http://www.fda.gov/forconsumers/consumerupdates/ucm151209.ht m (accessed March 6, 2010).

uval D, Giger U. " Vaccine associated immune-mediated hemolytic anaemia in the dog." *J Vet Intern Med*, 1996: 10:290-295.

Index

ACTH, 11, 58, 61

ACTH stimulation, 21, 22

Addisonian crisis, 56, 58

Addisonian reaction, 30, 57

adrenal cortex, 11, 58, 59, 61

Adrenal cortical tumor, 13

adrenal glands, 11, 56, 58, 61, 62

adrenal insufficiency, 56

adrenal tumors, 24

adrenocorticotropic hormone, 11, 58, 61

aldosterone, 11, 58, 62

alopecia, 16

American Veterinary Medical Association, 51

anestrus, 17

Anipryl. *See* 2. L-Deprenyl hydrochloride

atrial standstill, 58

Barrel stomach, 16

booster shots, 46, 47, 48

bradycardia, 56

capillary refill time, 59

Carbex. *See* 2. L-Deprenyl hydrochloride

cardiovascular collapse, 58

compounding pharmacies, 53

cortisol, 57, 58, 61, 62

Cortisol, 10, 11, 59

Diabetes Mellitus, 35

DNA, 40, 41, 42

Eldepryl. *See* 2. L-Deprenyl hydrochloride

electrolyte changes, 58

electrolytes, 54

Enlarged liver (hepatomegaly), 16

Florinef, 52, 54

genes, 40, 41, 45

genetics, 40, 41

glucocorticoid, 59

Hair loss (alopecia). *See* Alopecia

hyperadrenocorticism, 10, 16, 35

hypoadrenocorticism, 56

hypocortisolism, 56

hyponatremia, 58

Hypophysectomy, 35

hypovolemia, 58

Iatrogenic (veterinarian-induced), 13, 21

Ketoconazole, 25, 31, 61

kidneys, 10, 34, 57, 58

L-Deprenyl hydrochloride, 25, 26

Make A Wish, 55

Mitotane, 25, 29

muscle atrophy, 17

Percorten-V, 52, 53, 54

Pfizer, 48

pituitary, 10, 11, 12, 13, 20, 21, 22, 25, 26, 27, 35, 61

Pituitary Dependent, 25

Pituitary Tumor, 12

potassium, 60, 61

prednisone, 52, 54

selegiline. *See* 2. L-Deprenyl hydrochloride

symptoms, 16, 17, 18, 30, 56, 57, 62

Thromboembolism, 18, 35

titer test, 49, 50, 51

treatment, cheaper options, 52

Trilostane, 25

vaccinations, 46, 47, 50

Vetoryl. *See* Trilostane